# All About Animals
## Horses

By Christina Wilsdon

Reader's Digest Young Families

# Contents

# Chapter 1
## A Horse Grows Up

### Wild Words

*A female horse is called a **mare**. A male horse is called a **stallion**. A baby horse is called a **foal** (rhymes with the word "goal"). If the foal is male, it is also known as a **colt**. A female foal is a **filly**.*

A foal is born with legs that are almost as long as its mother's legs.

**B**aby Horse struggled to get to his feet. He had just been born and was already eager to stand. He tried sticking out his front legs and pushing up with his hind legs. Whoops! Baby Horse lost his balance and tumbled forward onto his nose. He landed gently in the thick bed of straw that filled the stall in the barn.

Every time Baby Horse sat down with a plop, Mama Horse nuzzled him and licked his ears. Baby Horse rested for a few minutes. Then he tried to get up again.

Finally, Baby Horse stood shakily on his long, thin legs. He stretched his neck and reached underneath Mama Horse's belly to drink her warm milk.

Then Baby Horse slept. By morning he was able to stand and walk at Mama Horse's side in the pasture. Soon he was trotting and even running as fast as she was!

## Baby Steps

Learning to control its legs is tricky for a newborn foal! At first the foal wobbles and often topples over. But it is able to stand within an hour after birth.

Mama Horse spent many hours eating grass. While she grazed, Baby Horse played. He dashed about, bucking and kicking. He chased butterflies. Every now and then, he stopped to nurse.

Mama Horse liked to trot and gallop in the pasture. Baby Horse romped with her, keeping pace at her side. All this exercise tired him out. He took long naps in the grass, flat on his side with his legs stretched out.

The two horses lived on a farm, so Mama Horse did not need to worry about animals that might harm her baby. Her owner and the farm's guard dog were on duty. Fences and barns also protected them. Even so, Mama Horse was as watchful over her little one as any wild mare.

When he was a week old, Baby Horse and his mama joined the rest of the farm's horses in another field. The other horses were all mamas with babies. Suddenly Baby Horse had lots of playmates!

## Sleepy Time

A foal grows very quickly during its first few months of life. It also burns a lot of energy playing and must get lots of rest. A foal may spend half the day sleeping!

All foals, such as this Thoroughbred, like to trot alongside their mothers.

## Hands Up!

A horse's height is traditionally measured in units called hands. A hand equals four inches. It is based on the average size of a human hand. The horse's height is measured at the curved part of its back, right behind its neck.

When foals are six months old, they spend more time with other foals than with their moms.

The baby horses nipped at each other. They reared up on their hind legs and boxed with their front legs. They galloped to the fence and back again. They charged in circles around the grazing mares. They squealed and whinnied. They grew stronger with all this play.

Baby Horse met the people who lived on the farm. They came to visit the horses every day. Mama Horse always let the people pet her. Baby Horse knew he could trust the people, too. He did not like it the first time they put a halter on his head and tried to lead him. But he soon grew used to it.

When Baby Horse turns six months old, he will weigh almost half as much as his mother. By the time Baby Horse and his friends are four years of age, they will be all grown up and trained as riding horses.

## Horse Chow

Milk is a foal's main food for its first few months of life. By the time it is three months old, it is also eating grass and grain. A foal on a farm usually nurses until it is between four to six months old. In the wild, foals often nurse for a few months longer.

11

# Chapter 2
# The Body of a Horse

# On the Hoof

All horses have hooves. A hoof is actually the horse's toenail, and it is made of the same material as your nails. A one-toe hoof is a special feature of horses. Millions of years ago, the ancestors of horses had more toes. But over time, the other toes shrank or disappeared, which helped horses run faster to escape predators.

A horse's long legs are powered by strong muscles in the upper legs and body. The structure of a horse's leg helps to store energy and release it as the horse moves.

The length of a horse's legs helps it take long steps, or strides, and to run fast. Horses need to be fast runners because running is how they escape danger. A horse is able to outrun most other animals.

## Pony Only

A pony is a separate breed of horse that is smaller, shorter, and stockier than other horses. The legs of a pony are shorter than the legs of a horse.

With more than 200 breeds, or kinds, of horses, there's a huge variety in sizes, colors, and shapes.

## As Big as a Horse

The largest horse is the shire. A shire can be 5 ½ feet tall at the shoulder — about the height of an average adult. Some shires are even taller than that. The smallest horse is the Falabella. It is just 30 inches tall at the shoulder — a bit bigger than a German shepherd.

## Turning Gray

Most gray horses are born black and fade to gray as they grow. A gray horse may be practically white by the time it is old.

Appaloosa horses always have spotted coats. The spots range from a big patch over the rump to a body dotted from nose to tail. Appaloosas were originally bred by the Nez Perce Indians of North America.

# A Horse of Different Colors

Horses have an amazing range of colors. The colors are created by different shades of brown as well as black and white. A horse's coat of hairs can be all the same color or different colors.

A **gray** horse has a dark skin covered with a mixture of black and white hairs. If it has brown flecks, it is called a flea-bitten gray. A dapple-gray horse has circles of dark hair that make its coat look speckled.

A **white** horse usually has a cream-colored or very light gray coat over dark skin. A truly white horse has white hairs and pink skin.

A **black** horse's hairs are black, while a brown horse's coat is a mixture of brown and black hairs.

If a horse is **red-brown** with a black mane and tail, it is called a bay. A golden-brown horse with a golden-brown mane and tail is called a chestnut or a sorrel.

A **golden** horse with a white mane and tail is called a Palomino. A horse splashed with white patches is called a pinto or paint.

# Stars and Stripes

Horses may also have unique markings. A horse may have a white star, stripe, or blaze on its face. It may have a dark stripe down its back or a series of rings on its legs. Legs can also have white markings of different sizes, such as short white socks or long white stockings.

## Big Eyes

A horse has the largest eyes of any land mammal. Each eye measures up to two inches across.

A horse can even watch for danger when its head is lowered while grazing.

# Eating Like a Horse

For its size, a horse has a small stomach. A horse must eat small amounts of food often instead of a lot of food at one time. That is why a horse spends so much time grazing.

Wild horses survive on grass and other plants. Most tame horses are fed hay and grains to give them extra energy. A riding horse may need up to 8 pounds of grain a day plus 15 to 20 pounds of hay! A horse also drinks about 8 to 10 gallons of water a day, or more if it is working hard.

# High Sight

The eyes of a horse are set high on the sides of its head, which means it has a good view of the land around it. A horse can see far-away objects very clearly. It can also see close-up, though it often needs to tilt its head up and down to get a sharp image. But a horse can't see right under its nose. If you offer a horse part of an apple on the palm of your hand, it will snuffle with its nose and feel around with its soft lips and whiskers to find it.

## Straight From A Horse's Mouth

Young horses have 24 baby teeth. They are replaced with 36 to 44 permanent teeth. Chewing grass and hay wears down the surface of the teeth. But a horse's teeth keep pushing up through the gums until the horse is about 25 years old, so it always has new chewing surfaces ready to use.

# Chapter 3
# Horses in Motion

### Fox Trots!

Some breeds are named for their special gaits. The Missouri Fox Trotter horse looks as if it is walking with its front legs while trotting with its hind legs. The Tennessee Walking Horse does a running walk, which is a fast, smooth walk marked by extra-long strides.

A galloping horse is balanced on just one hoof during part of each stride. As it gets its legs ready for the next stride, a galloping horse has all four hooves off the ground for an instant!

# Giddy-Up!

*Clip-clop, clip-clop!* This four-beat sound is made by a horse as it walks. A walk is one of the horse's four natural ways of moving. These movements are called gaits. The other three gaits are the trot, canter, and gallop.

A **walk** is the horse's slowest gait. A walk can be as slow as the plodding of a pony taking a young child for a ride or faster than many humans can run!

A **trot** is a faster gait. A trotting horse makes a fast, two-beat *clop-clop* sound. It moves its right front leg and left rear leg forward at the same time when it trots. Then the other two legs move forward. The trot feels very bouncy to a beginning rider. A rider learns to move up and down as the horse trots. This motion is called posting.

A **canter** is a three-beat gait. A horse cantering slowly may not move as fast as a horse trotting very quickly. But a horse cantering swiftly may be on the verge of galloping!

A **gallop** is a very fast four-beat gait. A galloping horse stretches its legs and reaches out in long strides. A horse can gallop at a speed of about 30 miles an hour—about as fast as a car driving on a city street. A horse in a pasture may gallop just because it is full of energy.

# And They're Off!

The fastest horses of all are Thoroughbred racehorses. A Thoroughbred can gallop at 40 miles an hour. Some are even faster. A top racehorse can run a mile in a little over a minute and a half. But even a racehorse can't keep up this speed for long. Most horse races are a mile and a quarter or less in length. Thoroughbred racehorses are ridden by lightweight riders called jockeys. A jockey guides a horse through a race and saves its energy for a burst of speed at just the right time.

# Pacing and Racing

The Standardbred is famous for its pacing ability. A pace is a two-beat gait, like the trot, but faster. A pacing horse moves its right legs forward at the same time. Then it moves its two left legs forward. A Standardbred competes in a sport called harness racing in which it pulls a driver in a small cart at a fast speed.

## Horse Shoes

Horses that are ridden or driven on hard surfaces wear metal horseshoes to protect their hooves. The shoes stop the hooves from getting worn down. Each metal shoe is specially shaped to fit each hoof. The shoe is nailed to the hoof, which does not hurt the horse because the nails go into a part of the hoof that has no feeling. The shoes are replaced every six weeks.

Thoroughbreds are the fastest horses, but they can race at top speed for only about a mile. In a race, jockeys must judge when to urge their horses to run the fastest. Some races are won by "just a nose"!

Some horses are naturally good jumpers, but they still must spend hours practicing with their riders.

# Leaps and Bounds

Some horses are good jumpers. Top jumpers and their riders may compete in show-jumping competitions where the horses must jump over a series of fences and walls.

Horses that are show jumpers may face jumps that can be taller than they are! A rider must pace the horse so that it is able to leap at just the right moment to clear the jump. If the horse does not feel ready to leap, it may stop in its tracks in front of the jump. This is called refusing.

Riders and jumpers also go over fences and walls in cross-country events. These competitions are held on courses outdoors, not in show rings. Some horses even jump while racing against other horses on a track! A horse race with jumps in it is called a steeplechase.

# Yee-Haw!

Horses not only run and jump—they also buck! Bucking horses called "broncos" often kick up their heels at rodeos. At a rodeo, riders compete in events that feature skills used on cattle ranches, such as calf roping.

Barrel racing is an exciting event in which a horse gallops around steel drums as fast as it can. It shows off the fast moves that a "cow pony" needs when it helps round up cattle.

# Chapter 4
# Horses in Herds

Horses do not like to be alone. They are
social animals, which means they need to be
with other horses. This is clearly seen in a
band of wild horses.

# A Wild Bunch

A band of wild horses is usually made up of a stallion, a few mares, their foals, and some colts and fillies a year or two older than the foals.

The stallion's main job is to protect the mares and foals in his band from predators. Often he follows behind the band, protecting it from the rear. He also fights with any stallions who try to steal the mares or take over the band. The lead stallion mates with the mares in spring. He is the father of all the foals in the band.

A band also has a lead mare. All the other mares recognize her as the boss. The lead mare is often at the head of the band, with the other horses following her. She is the one who decides when the band will graze, drink, rest, and where it will go.

## Ear Full

Horses not only listen with their ears — they also "talk" with them! The position of a horse's ears shows how it is feeling. Pricked ears mean a horse is alert and listening. If its ears are pricked and the whites of its eyes are showing, it may be scared. Floppy ears mean the horse is very relaxed. But watch out for a horse with its ears flattened back against its head. This means anger. A horse with pinned-back ears is saying, "Stay back! Go away!"

# Baby Horses

In spring, a mare leaves the herd to give birth in a secret, safe place. It will take up to three days for her foal to bond with her and know that she is its mother. When the mare returns to the herd, she warns other mares to stay away from her foal. Keeping other mares away helps prevent her foal from getting confused.

In the wild, fillies and colts stay with their band until they are about three years old. By that time, their mothers have had one or two more foals.

A filly often chooses to leave the band on her own. She will seek out a new band or be rounded up by another stallion. But a three-year-old colt is driven away by the stallion. He is chased, bitten, and kicked until he gives up trying to rejoin the band. The colt joins a group of other colts, which is called a bachelor band. The colt stays in the bachelor band until he is ready to collect a band of mares of his own.

# A Grooming Buddy

A horse's best friend in the herd is often a grooming buddy. The pair stands side by side, facing in opposite directions. Then each horse nibbles up and down the other horse's back and neck. This shared grooming helps get rid of dirt and loose hair in places a horse can't reach by itself. Grooming is also the horses' way of strengthening their friendship.

Two horses, like these quarterhorses, sometimes stand nose to tail. They swish their tails back and forth to help one another shoo pesky flies.

## Up and Down

A horse lies down and rolls over on the ground to scratch its back. A horse may lie down to sleep, but it also can snooze while standing up! A horse locks its leg joints together to stay upright while it sleeps.

**Horses recognize one another by smell as well as by sight!**

# Horse Talk

The best-known horse sound is the neigh. It is a loud, ringing sound that can be heard from far away. Horses neigh to find out where other horses are. A whinny is a shorter, higher-pitched neigh. A horse whinnies to greet another horse and to let other horses know it is there.

A horse also makes a low, rumbling sound to say hello. This sound is called a nicker. Horses nicker to other horses and their riders. A horse may even nicker if it thinks food is on the way!

Other sounds include puffs, snorts, and squeals. A horse may puff gently through its nostrils when it greets another horse nose-to-nose. A loud snort through the nostrils means the horse is scared or excited. Play-fighting produces squeals. A horse may also squeal if it is annoyed.

# Body Language

Horses also use their bodies to send messages to other horses. Two stallions walk stiffly with necks and tails arched when they approach each other, as if trying to look tough. A stallion rounding up a mare lowers his neck and stretches out his head to signal that he wants her to move.

A horse may kick out with a front leg to say stay away. If it turns its rump toward the other horse, it may be about to kick with both hind legs! A foal avoids getting kicked by snapping its teeth to say, "I'm little and weak and won't hurt you."

# Chapter 5
# Horses in the World

A horse and rider move as a unit.
This relationship often grows and
deepens over years.

# People and Horses

Early humans hunted wild horses for food. About 6,000 years ago, people in parts of Asia and Europe began to keep herds of horses. They may have used them for milk and meat. Nobody knows just when someone first thought of climbing onto a horse's back and riding it or hitching it to a cart. But pictures and items from ancient cultures show that people have been using horsepower for at least 4,000 years.

Ever since, horses have played an important role in human history. Knights and other warriors rode horses into battle. Explorers brought them to North America and South America. Travelers rode horses or sat in horse-drawn carriages to move to other places. Horses pulled plows and other machinery on farms as well as wagons full of goods from farms to cities.

## Heave, Ho!

Big workhorses are called draft horses or heavy horses. The giant horses that carried knights into battle long ago are the ancestors of some breeds of draft horses. Draft horses are still used to pull wagons and plows in some places. Some horses also compete in horse-pulling contests in which teams pull loads weighing thousands of pounds.

# Horses in the Wild

There are about 60 to 65 million horses in the world today. Most are tame, or domestic, horses. The others are wild horses. The ancestors of many of these wild horses are domestic horses that escaped or were set free long ago. Such horses are often called "feral" horses.

Feral horses have different names in different places. The wild horses of the western United States are called mustangs. Their ancestors include horses that were ridden by Spanish explorers and Native Americans. In Australia, feral horses are called brumbies.

## Fast Facts About Horses

| | |
|---|---|
| Scientific name | *Equus caballus* |
| Class | Mammalia |
| Order | Perissodactyla |
| Size | Up to 6 feet at the shoulder |
| Weight | Up to 2,200 pounds |
| Life span | 25 to 30 years |
| Habitat | Grasslands (in the wild) Pastures (domestic) |
| Speed | About 40 miles per hour |

## Spirit Horses

The wild horse of Mongolia is thought to be the world's only "true" wild horse because its ancestors were never tamed. It is also called Przewalski's horse. The Mongolian people call it the *takhi,* which means "spirit" in their language.

Mustangs get their name from the Spanish word *mestena*, which means "herd."

# Glossary of Wild Words

**bachelor band** a group of male horses

**bay** a horse with a red-brown coat and black mane and tail

**blaze** a white streak down the center of a horse's face

**breed** a specific kind of animal

**canter** a three-beat gait that is between a trot and a gallop in speed

**colt** a male foal or young horse

**draft horse** a very large horse used for heavy work

**feral** living in the wild and no longer tame

**filly** a female foal or young horse

**foal** a baby horse

| | | | |
|---|---|---|---|
| **gait** | a horse's leg motion | **species** | a group of living things that are the same in many ways |
| **gallop** | a four-beat running gait | | |
| **mare** | an adult female horse | **stallion** | an adult male horse |
| **pace** | a two-beat gait in which the horse moves both legs on one side of its body at the same time | **stocking** | a long white marking on a horse's leg |
| | | **trot** | a two-beat gait that is faster than a walk |
| **sock** | a short white marking on a horse's leg | | |

# Index